HOW TO BE ON TOP

by living in

BLISS FOREVER

FIND INSIDE

Gyanesh Chaudhry

BEEJA
HOUSE

ISBN: 978-81-19682-94-2 (Hardback)

978-81-19682-55-3 (Paperback)

Published by: Beeja House

Printed By: Repro India Pvt. Ltd.

First Printing Edition 2023

Author Email: beejgyanc@gmail.com

DEDICATION

This work is dedicated to, highly respected and eminent, my late parents - Shri Des Raj Chaudhry and Smt. Chandra Vati, both were freedom fighters and prominent Social Workers of Delhi. They managed and set up many philanthropic institutions in Delhi; and from whom I learned many lessons of life, most important and useful being —

1. Always keep learning and rising; and develop your own ability so as to be able to stand on your own legs.
2. Always serve and help the needy.
3. Be selfless.
4. Have full faith in the Almighty.

May their noble souls rest in eternal peace at the feet of the Almighty

I sincerely hope this book will benefit and help every reader. May the Almighty be ever with you all, bestowing the best of health, ever-lasting happiness, joy and peace and surrounding you with the right people.

May you be blessed with the
Divine Grace forever and the
Almighty be always with you.

PREFACE

This book is based on learning and own experiences of the author during his lifetime to get positive and good results by the grace of the Almighty. It has been brought — out with the expectation that the reader could gain immensely from it provided she/he has a strong will to learn, practice and adopt earnestly the procedure advised. It would lead to a positive mental transformation to provide grand results for the reader. It would bring happiness and joy to the reader, besides manifold progress in life.

It is advised, before practicing, to go through the procedure a couple of times mentally to get used to it. Follow it with full faith and the **Almighty will surely get you the desired good results.**

May you and your loved ones
be always well, healthy, happy,
full of joy, and surrounded by
good and right people.

Gyanesh Chaudhry
27 November 2023
New Delhi

ACKNOWLEDGEMENT

The author expresses his deep gratitude to the Gurus/teachers who taught "Meditation and Getting the Desired Results", viz.

i. Silva Hose Course conducted in Delhi by Mr. Bimol Rakshit in the late 1980s - a big thank you, Sir.

ii. SSY (Sidh Samadhi Yoga) Course of late Shri Rishi Prabhakar of Bangalore, conducted in Delhi in January 1994 under Dr. Indrani - ex Maths Prof of IIT Bombay. I am highly obliged to you, Ma'am.

I would also like to thank Ms. Pearl Drego of TACET New Delhi for teaching, in the early 1980s TA (Transactional Analysis), very useful for interpersonal relationships.

And lastly, but most importantly, I am indebted to my wife, Achla, without whose constant support and encouragement, this work would not have been possible.

CONTENTS

CHAPTER ONE

Get Bliss Now

Discovering the Path to Instant Joy

What is bliss? It's a question that has intrigued philosophers, poets, and seekers of truth for centuries. Some have described it as a state of supreme happiness, while others have likened it to an inner contentment that transcends the fleeting pleasures of life. But in its essence, bliss is a deeply personal and profoundly transformative experience.

At the age of 79, as I sit down to write this book, I can attest that bliss is not a distant, unattainable dream. It is not a reward reserved only for the fortunate or the spiritually enlightened. Bliss is, in fact, a state of being that each one of us has the potential to embrace and nurture.

In this chapter, we shall embark on a journey of understanding, where we explore the very essence of bliss. We shall peel back the layers of complexity and discover that bliss is not a complex puzzle; it is a fundamental aspect of our human existence. It is the state of being in harmony with ourselves and the world around us.

Bliss is not merely the absence of suffering or the fleeting pleasure of material gains. It is a profound sense of inner peace, a feeling of contentment that arises when we align with the natural flow of life. It is the serenity that accompanies us even in the face of adversity.

What Is Bliss?

Many people spend their lifetime seeking "bliss". But where to find bliss and how?

Bliss is a state of extreme happiness and utmost joy. It is a deep and profound sense of well-being. Bliss is often associated with moments of great pleasure or fulfillment, and it can be experienced in various aspects of life, such as in personal relationships, achievements, or even in simple, serene moments of peace and tranquility.

The phenomenon is often co-related in terms of philosophical, religious, and spiritual contexts to describe a state of utmost happiness, enlightenment, or union with a higher power or the universe.

However, everyone has anxieties, worries and tensions regarding home, professional life, loved ones, etc. and is seeking happy solutions to various problems.

In that case, how to have mental peace and relaxation? Here it is **HOW!** By following **Mental Exercise.**

One of the suitable and many methods given here. Doing it may take about 15 to 20 minutes.

Suggestion: please go through the procedure given below a couple of times and try to register it in your mind. ***Do not worry*** you don't have to remember it.

The procedure may be practiced repeatedly till it becomes a normal routine. Please follow as given below:

Choose a quiet place or corner where you can sit without any disturbance. No phone, no mobile, and no doorbells. Tell your people around there not to disturb you **unless there is FIRE or some other danger.**

Sit comfortably on a chair with a soft cushion as a backrest, keeping your spine vertical and straight. Feet resting on the floor flat or crossed as comformtable, insulated from the earth through a mat, carpet, cotton sheet, or wooden plank to enable you to retain the electrical energy in your body. Place your two palms one over the other in your lap. **OR** place your hands on your knees with palms facing downwards as convenient. Close your eyes gently and they will remain closed during the rest of this exercise.

Physically, now you are at rest and comfortable. Be at ease totally.

Relax mentally. Visualize your favorite flowers in full colors, with pretty butterflies flying around. Be in a happy state.

Now ask yourself gently: "What is bothering me the most? And what is the worst that can happen?" Even if it happens (it won't happen as you will see in a minute), you lose nothing as it all belongs to God - so He loses if at all! But God can't lose. Hence, just relax, nothing is going to be lost. Leave this worry and anxiety to Him and **you be free**.

✓ **ASSERT**: “We all are created by the Almighty who is our Father. No father would ever let any harm come to his children. Hence, no harm would come to me or my family. We all are under

His continuous observation and total protection. My any loss or profit is His, not mine."

Feel His **all-ness and one-ness** with you.

Further say, "I don't want to harm anybody nor have any such intention. Hence, no harm could come to me or my loved ones."

The Almighty has created this universe in **total harmony** all around. So, it would be around us – total harmony.

The Almighty loves His creation which is under His full security and protection. Hence, **we are under His total protection and guidance.**

And lo! **You are now happy and full of joy AND mentally free totally. Leave all the worry and anxiety to God and He would take care of it all. Have full Trust and Faith in Him.**

Belief In God

If you, or anyone else, do not believe in God, consider this:

Can you choose:

(i) The time of coming to or leaving this world?
(ii) Your parents?
(iii) Your brothers/sisters or children?

The answer is 'No' to all of the above; neither you nor can anyone else.

There is an invisible force that determines it, and it is called **God or Almighty or Creator or Supreme being!**

Some call it 'Nature'! And who controls it? **The Supreme-being.**

Now, **firmly establish in your mind – your belief in God. Thank the Father for giving you all you have.**

If you have a Deity (Devi or Devta), in whom you have full trust and faith, recall it **mentally** and visualize it in its full Form and Color. Bow to it and pray:

> *"Prabhu (or O Lord), kindly protect me, my family and my loved ones from all evils and support us with good solutions to all our problems. Kindly be with us all the while and guide us to take the right path. Please surround us with the right people. Thank you, Father."*

And lo! **All your tensions melt away and are gone. You are now in BLISS.** Feel it and enjoy it. Visualize being at your favorite beautiful place and enjoying its surroundings.

Smile. Open your eyes gently. Relax. You may be feeling tired or sleepy. Take a nap. Wake up smiling and feeling fresh.

As you will open your eyes you will feel:

- **Calmness**: The practice can help reduce stress and anxiety, leading to a feeling of relaxation and tranquility.

- **Clarity of Mind**: You may find that your thoughts are more organized, and you can think more clearly.

- **Reduced Stress**: It will lead to a reduction in the physical and emotional symptoms of stress.

- **Increased Awareness**: It will enhance your self-awareness and mindfulness, making you more attuned to your thoughts, emotions, and sensations.

- **Improved Mood:** It will help regulate emotions and promote a positive outlook.

- **Relaxation**: It will induce a deep state of relaxation, which can lead to feelings of physical and mental well-being.

- **Sense of Connection:** It will lead to a feeling of connection to a higher power, the universe, the Divine Medium or a sense of oneness with all things.

You have undergone a process of mental transformation.

Now you have:	**NO** tension at all nor anxiety or any worry on any account whatsoever.
	You will be now **Relaxed, Happy, and Joyous.** Such a state of mind, will get you the best solutions of your problems.
	Have full **Faith and Trust** in the Almighty who would surely lead you to the right actions and thereby good solutions.

You have to adhere to it AND remain in continuous touch and contact with your Deity or Lord. Pray before each meal, 3 times daily for 5 minutes: The prayer given below would take just a couple of minutes. Close your eyes and think of the Almighty.

"Dear Prabhu/Lord: Kindly protect me, my family and my loved ones from all evils; and guide us to take the right path for better and higher levels of healthy and happy living. Please surround us with the right people.

Thank you, Father.

Never ever give up praying. Be in constant touch with the Almighty and communicate with Him, and He will look after you fully.

☆ ☆ ☆

"Bliss is not a destination; it's a state of being to be embraced and adopted forever.

CHAPTER TWO

To Be In Bliss Forever

Unlocking the Secrets to Lasting Happiness

In the ancient epic, the Mahabharata, there is a tale of Lord Krishna, the divine incarnation and his visit to the court of the powerful King Yudhishthira. During this visit, King Yudhishthira posed a question to Lord Krishna, seeking to understand the nature of true happiness and contentment. In response, Lord Krishna placed a single grain of rice on one side of a scale and all the wealth of the kingdom on the other. Astonishingly, the grain of rice outweighed all the riches.

The message of this story is clear: true wealth, the ultimate treasure, is found not in material possessions but in the wealth of inner bliss. It is this inner wealth that we shall continue to explore in this chapter, as we strive to uncover the secrets to being in bliss forever.

WHY Be In Bliss?

Bliss is not a fleeting emotion or a temporary state of elation. It is the foundation upon which we can build the best state of living—a life of maximum happiness and utmost joy. But the benefits of bliss extend far beyond mere happiness. It is also a powerful catalyst for:

B : *Best state of living* - of maximum Happiness and utmost Joy.

L : *Longevity* - A happy mind contributes to sound health, leading to a longer and more fulfilling life.

I : *Illness prevention* - With a perpetually content and joyful state of mind, we fortify ourselves against the afflictions of illness, paving the way for a disease-free existence.

S : *Satisfaction and contentment* - Bliss allows us to lead a life filled with satisfaction and contentment, all the while continually progressing toward our goals.

S : *Smiles* - It bestows upon us the gift of an ever-present smile, radiating the warmth of our inner self to the world.

However, to truly experience and maintain this state of cool and calm, there are three vital factors we must ensure in our lives:

1. **Health** - A sound body is the temple of a blissful mind. We shall explore practices and habits that nurture physical well-being, allowing us to thrive in a state of serenity.

2. **Finance** - Financial stability and prosperity are crucial components of a blissful life. We shall

delve into practical strategies for achieving financial stability without succumbing to the anxieties of materialism.

3. **Interpersonal Relationships** - Our connections with others are the tapestry of our existence. We shall uncover the secrets to nurturing harmonious and enriching relationships that contribute to our lasting state of bliss.

Let us master these three elements to ensure that happiness is not a fleeting visitor but a permanent resident of our lives.

Health

Your health is what matters the most, for as they say, "*Health is Wealth*". It is not just a proverb but a learning that emphasizes the importance of good health as one of the most valuable assets in life. Good health is paramount as it leads to longevity, good quality of life and continual elation - mental well-being leads to energy, vitality and resilience.

Take care of your own health and of your loved ones. **If there is any health issue or of someone close to you, do not ignore** it. Get the best possible medical attention right away to get rid of the problem permanently. In your daily prayers, request the Almighty/your Deity to guide you toward a permanent cure for the problem.

To attain and preserve good health, it's important to inculcate a balanced and holistic approach that includes regular physical activity, a nutritious diet, adequate sleep, stress management, and regular medical check-ups. Prioritizing your health is an investment in your overall well-being and can lead to a more rewarding and fulfilling life.

As per the **Health Experts**, for good and sound health one should have **REGULAR** hours for:

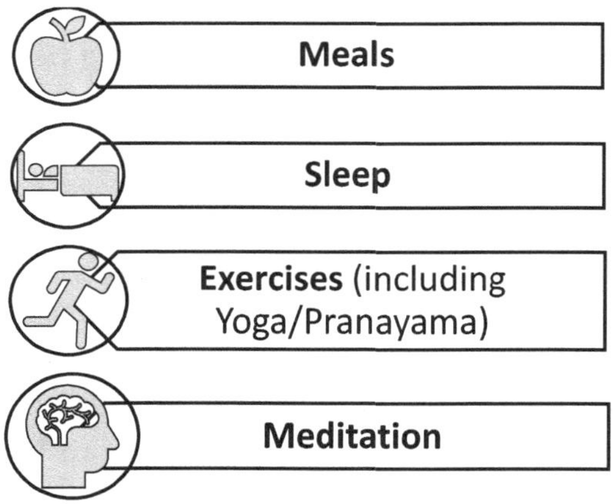

Experts suggest (rightly) that:

At 36 years of age (or later earliest), please adopt such a physical exercise pattern that you would be easily able to follow daily, and continue to do even at the age of 60 and beyond.

- **Brisk walking daily for 45 minutes**
  OR
- **Walking on Tread Mill daily, 4.5 Km.**

AND combine it with 15-20 minutes of Pranayama and Yoga; and at least 30 minutes (15 minutes, 2 times) of **Meditation** daily. Total of 45+20+30 = 95 minutes.

It would keep you fit and agile and your surroundings happy and joyous.

Cycling, swimming, rope-skipping or tennis becomes difficult to do later as one advances in age.

Now for a minimum of **30 minutes of meditation daily** - ***how to find time?*** Time would be available to you. We are going to do **Magic.** Keep reading, please.

As one starts doing meditation twice daily for at least 15 minutes each time, there is a surprise in store!

The sleeping time of the doer goes down itself by two hours.

And there is no tiredness nor sleepiness. Two hours less 30 minutes of meditation – you are still left with 1 and 1/2 hours of extra time! So, there is time gain. Magic – isn't it?

To start with, the best time advised for beginners for *Meditation* is:

For 15 minutes before breakfast and dinner each.

You may re-schedule or adjust your overall activities to fit everything snugly.

Finance

Managing your finances is crucial as it directly impacts your living, mental well-being, stability, and future prospects. Funds and money are pivotal aspects for everyone. Its smooth in-flow and out-flow every week or month for necessary expenses would ensure hassle-free operations.

But why is it important?

- **Financial Stability:** Effective financial management helps you maintain stability in your (*financial*) life. It ensures that you have enough money to cover your regular expenses and can handle unexpected financial challenges.

- **Debt Management**: Proper financial management allows you to control and reduce debt. It helps you avoid accumulating high-interest debt, which can be financially crippling.

- **Savings and Investments:** Managing your finances enables you to save and invest for the future. This can include building an emergency fund, saving for major life goals (e.g., education, home ownership, retirement), and investing to grow your wealth.

- **Financial Security:** Managing your finances provides a sense of financial security. You have a safety net in case of unexpected expenses, job loss, or other financial setbacks.

- **Peace of Mind:** Knowing that you are in control of your finances can reduce stress and provide peace of mind. You don't have to constantly worry about money-related issues.

- **Emergency Preparedness:** Financial management prepares you for unexpected emergencies, such as medical bills, car repairs, or home repairs. It ensures you have the resources to handle these situations.

- **Financial Independence:** Effective financial management can help you achieve financial independence. You can make choices based on your values and goals rather than being dependent on others for financial support.

- **Building Wealth:** By managing your finances wisely, you can accumulate wealth over time. This wealth can provide opportunities and financial security for you and your family.

So, do plan, monitor, and ensure it, thereby making your life easy and happy.

But what if you face trouble while preparing for it?

Well, for any problem in any area, you may be surprised to get its solution through **meditation** and by

praying to your Deity or the Almighty. There are some suggestions and tips given below to help you to be **in Bliss** all the while:

✓ Always have full trust and faith in the Almighty.

✓ Always be cool and calm under all circumstances. Just keep smiling (difficult though in the beginning). If the situation is disturbing, don't say or express anything- just smile and let it pass. The right solution will come to your mind sooner or later. Then handle it and carry it out peacefully.

✓ Always be polite, yet firm, all the while. It would be possible eventually after repeated practice.

✓ Keep a diary and a pen near your bedside. Before sleeping, review the happenings of the day; and note down all disturbing situations. Were you cool and calm? Now close your eyes gently and mentally assert to always remain cool.

✓ Always have a positive attitude and outlook in all matters, however bad the situation may appear to be. Remember the Almighty and leave all the worries and solutions to Him.

✓ Relax and smile.

Interpersonal Relationships

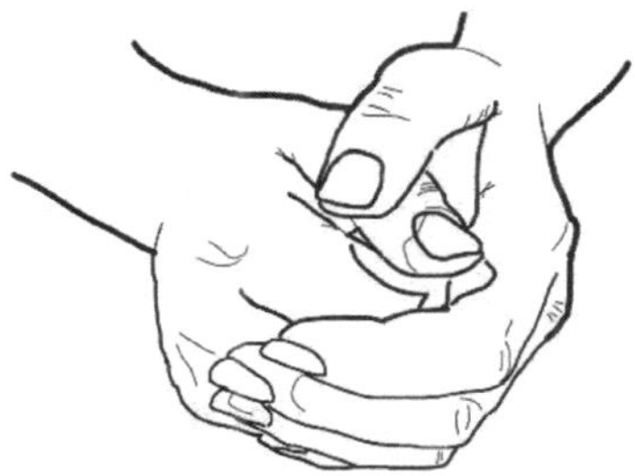

When you forge connections and relations with different individuals, you build interpersonal relationships. These relationships are a fundamental aspect of human life and are characterized by various forms of social bonds, communication, and emotional connections between people. However, if any ripple erupts in relationships it leads to mental agony and displeasure. It, in turn, disrupts your bliss.

With a few steps, you can achieve a state of bliss in your interpersonal relationships. How? Let's see!

1. **Effective Communication:** Open, honest, and empathetic communication is the foundation of strong relationships. Listen actively, express your thoughts and feelings clearly, and encourage others to do the same. Effective communication fosters understanding and connection.

2. **Empathy and Understanding**: Put yourself in the shoes of the other person and try to

understand his/her perspective, feelings, and needs. Empathy creates a sense of emotional connection and fosters trust.

3. **Quality Time:** Spend quality time with the people you care about. Give your full attention and be present in the moment when you're with them. Engage in activities that you both enjoy and that strengthen your bond.

4. **Appreciation and Gratitude:** Express your appreciation and gratitude for the people in your life. Regularly acknowledge their contributions and the positive impact they have on your well-being. Simple gestures of gratitude can go a long way.

5. **Boundaries**: Set clear and healthy boundaries in your relationships. Boundaries help define what is acceptable and what is not, ensuring that both parties feel respected and comfortable.

6. **Conflict Resolution:** Conflicts are a natural part of relationships. Approach conflicts with a problem-solving mindset, focusing on finding solutions rather than assigning blame. Effective conflict resolution can strengthen a relationship.

7. **Forgiveness**: Learn to forgive and let go of past grievances. Holding onto grudges can damage a

relationship. Forgiveness allows you to move forward with a clean slate.

8. **Support and Encouragement:** Be a source of support and encouragement for the people you care about. Offer assistance, encouragement, and emotional support when they face challenges or pursue their goals.

9. **Balance**: Maintain a healthy balance between your personal life and your relationships. It's important to have your own interests, goals, and self-identity while also nurturing your relationships.

10. **Grow Together:** Encourage personal growth and development in your relationships. Support each other's goals and aspirations, and be willing to adapt and grow together as you both change over time.

11. **Express Love:** Show love and affection through both words and actions. Small acts of kindness and expressions of love can contribute to the bliss in your relationships.

12. **Patience**: Building deep, blissful relationships takes time. Be patient and allow your connections to develop and evolve naturally.

The eminence and nature of interpersonal relationships can have a profound impression on a person's well-being and overall quality of life. Strong and positive relationships can provide emotional support, happiness, and a sense of belonging, while unhealthy relationships can be a source of stress and emotional turmoil. With commitment, effort, and the right mindset, you can foster blissful and fulfilling interpersonal relationships that bring joy and satisfaction to your life.

☆ ☆ ☆

"Lasting happiness is not a distant goal; it's right here, to be tuned-in mentally forever".

CHAPTER THREE

Meditation

The Inner Sanctuary of Bliss

In the hustle and bustle of our daily lives, we often find ourselves swept away by the currents of external demands and distractions. The modern world constantly bombards us with information, responsibilities, and the ceaseless chatter of the mind. In the midst of this chaos, we yearn for a sanctuary of serenity, a place where the mind can find solace and rediscover its true nature.

Welcome to Chapter 3, where we unlock the door to that inner sanctuary of bliss through the practice of meditation.

Meditation is not merely a trendy buzzword or a mystical pursuit reserved for ascetics in remote caves. It is a timeless and universal tool that can guide us toward the tranquil depths of our own consciousness. It is a journey inward, to a place where the noisy distractions of the world fade into the background, and we connect with the profound stillness that resides within.

In this chapter, we shall explore the art and science of meditation. We shall demystify this ancient practice and make it accessible to anyone seeking inner peace and clarity. Whether you are a beginner or have dabbled in meditation before, the insights and techniques shared here will help you deepen your practice and experience the profound benefits it offers.

Meditation is not a quick fix or a magic pill for all of life's challenges, but it is a powerful ally in our quest for lasting bliss. It has the potential to transform the way we perceive the world, our thoughts, and ourselves. It is a journey that can lead us to a state of unwavering inner calm, a space where bliss can flourish and expand.

So, as we step into the realm of meditation in this chapter, let go of any preconceived notions, open your heart and mind, and prepare to embark on a transformative journey into the sanctuary of your own being. The path to bliss begins within, and meditation is the key that unlocks the door to your inner sanctuary of serenity and joy.

Meditation Is A Boon To Humanity.

It provides the right course of action for the welfare and benefit of mankind. It gives happy solutions to our various troubles and problems. It is like a panacea for all ills.

It is a mental practice that involves focusing one's attention on a particular object, thought, sound, or activity to train awareness and achieve a mentally clear and emotionally calm state. It is a practice that has been around for thousands of years and is utilized for various purposes, including relaxation, stress reduction, self-awareness, and spiritual development.

MEDITATION is:

Mental
Exercise
Directly
Improves
Total
Anxieties and
Traumatic and other
Illnesses
Of
Natives.

It is a deep mental exercise to interact through our own subconscious mind with the **Divine Medium (DM). DM** is like an ocean of infinite wisdom and intelligence. It is present everywhere and encompasses the whole universe. It provides happy solutions to all problems, and it may even create favorable circumstances for you to solve your problem. Through meditation, one can approach and be a part of the **DM.**

Important

Please note that our ancient sages and saints who taught us meditation cautioned us not to discuss nor tell our experiences of meditation with anybody except, maybe, our Guru if essential or if he asks.

Before we were taught meditation, our Guru asked us to take a pledge that we would never stop doing meditation daily and do it at least twice every day. The same is expected of you, dear Reader. Please take the pledge and affirm 3 times in your mind with your eyes closed:

> *"I shall do meditation at least twice daily for the rest of my life."*

In order to get and enjoy the benefits of meditation, the following requisites are advised for the meditator:

- ✓ Always have a **positive** attitude for everything, even if the situation is bad – be hopeful and keep smiling.
- ✓ Carry **NO ill will** against anybody – forgive and forget.
- ⊗ Never have any intention or plan of causing any harm to anybody in any way.
- ✓ Always help others in whatever way possible.

> **Remember**: *We and all human beings sometimes or others commit mistakes and errors in life unintentionally. Let us forgive and forget it all and go forward in life happily.*

Hereby, forgive all who have disturbed or upset you in the past; and carry no malice or any grudge towards anyone.

> **Remember:** *To err is human, to forgive – divine.*

NOW **To Meditate**:

As advised in Chapter 1, sit comfortably on a chair with cozy and straight back support, keeping the spine vertical. Feet resting on the ground but insulated from Mother Earth through a mat, carpet, or cushion to prevent your body's electrical energy from going to the earth. Keep palms one over the other in your lap. Ensure no ring, no bell around, or any disturbance. Tell the people around you not to disturb you and make no noise at all unless there is . . . **FIRE or some other danger**.

Sitting Position For Meditation

Please sit facing **South, so the East - the direction of the rising sun, i.e., the future — is on your left.** We want favorable results from the meditation. The morning sun rising in the East daily brings new hopes for the future. Therefore, during meditation, sit facing South with the East on your left for the future. This is to visualize desired results or events happening on your left in the future.

During meditation with eyes closed, imagine a plane about 15° higher from your forehead, and look straight at it. Now visualize in **BLUE FRAME** on the plane the situation that you want to correct or improve. For example, your friend Mr. X smokes and you want him to give up smoking. Visualize in the Blue Frame your friend smoking. Now shift your vision mentally to the left (East) of the blue frame to a **BRIGHT WHITE** frame in which Mr. X is throwing away cigarettes and not smoking. So, a **bright white frame** is for the happy result desired by you. By doing this repeatedly in your meditation sessions, the desired result would come through. One by one, you can visualize your current problems in the **blue frame**. And the desired happy solution on its left in the bright **white frame** like happy weddings of your loved ones; various successes, loans being returned, winning of legal cases, gains in your profession and the like.

Facing the South direction while meditating would be initially required till you get accustomed to meditation. Later, when you are able to meditate easily anywhere, you may sit facing any direction with the **blue frame in front (to visualize the problem) and the bright white frame on its left. (To visualize the happy solution).**

Duration Of Meditation

Before starting, tell yourself mentally how much duration of meditation (or *Dhyayaan*) you want, say, 15 minutes. (Please keep 15-20 minutes in the beginning). It gets registered in your mind and body clock by itself, and it will surely bring you out of your meditative sleep (wake you up) after 15 minutes or the desired time!

It may not happen in the beginning, but, be sure, it does happen. However, keep a suitable time clock in your direct view in front of you. If you wake up or come out of the meditation before 15 minutes, close your eyes and go back to it. And, if you come out of it after 15 minutes, there is no problem – it is good. Just relax.

You have decided your time and fixed it in your mind. You are seated comfortably. Now, gently close your eyes. Remember the Almighty:

> *"Dear Om Prabhu (or Dear Lord), please solve my problems and clear my troubles. (State briefly your problems and troubles.) Please, Father, keep intact my prestige and position which are yours too. Thank you."*

Be sure and mentally relaxed. It would happen. Feel the Almighty's presence with you. The way Vedic Chants, Om, Mantras, Shlokas, or *Bhajans* (devotional songs) create positive vibrations in our cells, body, and mind. It is the same way it would be with you now. Have no doubt nor any tension nor any worry. You are in a semi-conscious state and in direct touch with the Supreme being.

Try to go into deeper meditation. To reach this state, please focus, with eyes closed, your eyes internally on:

- **Either the tip of your nose**
  OR
- **In between your eyebrows**.

Choose one place of the above two forever whichever you find easy. Various thoughts would be flowing in your mind. Just relax. Let them flow freely.

Don't try to stop them or chase any of them. Be totally relaxed; and continue focusing. Auto-suggest to yourself: I'm going deeper and deeper in meditation; deeper and deeper; deeper and deeper; deeper and deeper...

And lo! Without knowing it, you would soon be in deep meditative sleep and your mind would turn blank.

After the stipulated time as you decided in the beginning (15 minutes presently), you would wake up and come to consciousness.

Significant And Important

Please note this period of coming out of deep sleep is a **very crucial moment** - nature fulfills your wish for this moment provided it is not going to harm anybody.

After repeated meditation for 7-10 days, when you are able to regularly meditate, firmly fix your time for meditation daily, at least twice a day morning and evening, for 15 minutes each time. Follow it meticulously whether you are at home or the office or traveling in a motor car or bus, train, or plane. If in a hotel or restaurant, sit aside for 15 minutes and tell people around you not to disturb you and that you are going to meditate (*Dhyaan*) and will wake up by yourself.

Enjoy its Magic

So, you decide in the beginning what wish you want to get fulfilled this day; it could be about you or your loved one, regarding health, work, profession or anything else. Think a lot about it repeatedly and keep it in your mind for a few days; so that it stays in your mind and comes to your mind at the **crucial moment** as given above. After repeated practice, it would start happening.

When you wake up, before opening your eyes, thank the Almighty and request Him to be always with you, protecting and guiding you.

Reap the Benefits

- Reduced stress and anxiety by getting desired results ans solutions.
- Improved focus and attention.
- Enhanced emotional well-being and self-awareness.
- Better sleep quality.
- Increased relaxation and a sense of inner peace.
- Potential health benefits, including lower blood pressure and improved immune system function.
- Enhanced self-control and management of emotions.

> **CAUTION:** *Do not discuss results with anyone - not even with your spouse or the beneficiary nor with anyone else. You may, however, mention to them that you are going to pray for them.*

Best Wishes. May the Almighty
be always with you fulfilling
all your wishes and desires.

☆ ☆ ☆

"In the stillness of meditation, we find the clarity to navigate happily in life's turbulent waters."

CHAPTER FOUR

The Creator

Connecting with the Divine Source

In the grand tapestry of existence, there is a thread that weaves through the very fabric of our lives—an eternal, omnipresent force that transcends time and space. It is the thread that connects us to the source of all creation, the wellspring of boundless wisdom and compassion.

The Creator.

Throughout the ages, humanity has sought to understand and connect with this supreme, transcendent power. We have created myths, legends, and religions to capture the essence of the Creator, each culture and tradition offering its own unique perspective. In Hinduism, we find a rich and profound understanding of the divine—a belief that the Creator is not distant and aloof but an ever-present, loving presence that permeates all of creation.

Having traversed the corridors of life, I can attest to the transformative power of this belief. My spirituality has been a guiding light, a source of strength, and a wellspring of wisdom throughout my journey. I have come to realize that our connection to the Creator is not confined to the rituals of temples or the words of scriptures; it is a living, breathing relationship that can infuse our lives with purpose, meaning, and, yes, bliss.

The profound concept of the Creator and our understanding of this divine force can lead us to a deeper, more meaningful experience of life.

As we embark on this exploration of the Creator, I invite you to open your heart and mind to the infinite possibilities that lie before us. Let us peel back the layers of separation and rediscover the divine tapestry that connects us all. The Creator is not a distant figure to be worshipped from afar, but a loving presence that invites us to partake in the boundless bliss of existence.

Let's Go Back To The Start.

When we are born, we hardly know anything. As we grow, we start recognizing people around us – our parents, brothers, sisters, etc. We start going to school, maybe reluctantly, and make friends. And the charming teachers there play with us and try to make us learn a thing or two.

It is this time or thereabouts that we start wondering 'What is this all around?' and 'How did I come here?' Most of us ask our mothers: How did I come here? And why am I here?

In the answers, the concept of

God – The Supreme- being/the Almighty/the Creator

emerges and creeps into our little minds. We start wondering about this invisible entity! *Is it there and real? What does it look like? How can I meet Him?*

How is it so powerful? Where did it come from? Who made it? Can it give us lots of sweets and chocolates?

The concept of God as the creator provides a foundation for moral and ethical codes, the meaning and purpose of human life, and the understanding of divine providence. It also invites profound questions about the nature of suffering and the human relationship with the divine.

We learn that God has no beginning and no end and is perennial. It does not sink in. We don't believe it or understand it! However, as we grow, gradually the truth dawns on us.

We see and learn about the sun, moon, stars, sky, sea and its tides, various animals, birds, plants, trees, fruits, flowers, and the amazing honeybees, etc. We are told and made to understand that it is all created by God. He is omniscient and omnipotent. We grow and mature. We think we know a lot now. Later, we realize that what we know is not even a drop in the ocean.

God is a big mystery, and everyone might imagine God a little differently. Some people pray to God and feel close to God in special places like churches, mosques, or temples. These are like meeting spots where people can talk to God, just like you might talk to your best friend.

We learn about the theory of Karma and deeds. And that we get the **Fruits - sweet, sour, or bitter** - of our deeds (karmas) of our past lives. It is a fundamental principle that refers to the law of cause and effect, where one's actions have consequences, and these consequences can affect a person's current life and future lives.

Our deeds **with REAL INTENTIONS** attitudes and outlooks are all known to God. You can't hide anything from Him.

Do you have the sincere intention of selfless help and service in a performed deed or is it to seek some reward or return?

And your real intentions get known to Him. HOW?

Everything is in your subconscious mind which is linked to your soul. The Almighty has full access to it and hence knows your real intentions fully.

As you sow, so shall you reap.

Further, God helps those who help themselves and ***He helps those who help others too.***

Regardless of events and results, if your intentions are pure and good, the Creator goes with you all the way to get you the desired results.

The Creator is –

An ocean of
Infinite Wisdom
and Intelligence,
say the

Divine Medium (DM).

Divine Medium encompasses the whole universe. You can access it through meditation. It provides solutions to your all problems.

The Almighty has created us all, this world, and the universe. He loves His creations. He looks after us. He wants us to serve the underprivileged and humanity. When we ask Him for favors, He does give and provides the best solutions. Let's try to get one drop from His ocean which would do wonders for all our needs, problems, and troubles. One can remain in contact with Him through **meditation** and He takes care of everything.

The Creator has several attributes and volumes can be written about them. Here, however, only His all-knowing feature and His kindness as our Father are narrated briefly for living a good and meaningful life.

Understanding our **CREATOR** is like exploring a treasure map with different paths leading to unique destinations. People have their own beliefs, and that's what makes the world so diverse and interesting. No matter how people see God, the most important thing is that the idea of God often leads them to be better, more compassionate, and loving individuals. So, whether you have faith or not, the idea of God is a big part of our world, teaching us to be kind and make the world a better place. It's an idea that has been with humans for a very long time, and it continues to shape the way we live and interact with one another.

*"Faith in God gives
Meaning and Purpose
to Human life"*

PS. *Do meditate daily at least twice and remain in constant touch with Him. Constantly serve humanity and enjoy living. Be in bliss. Choose people around you and of your company very carefully – they should be sincere and honest. Meditation can guide you in selecting the right people.*

*May God bless you and
always guide you.*

☆ ☆ ☆

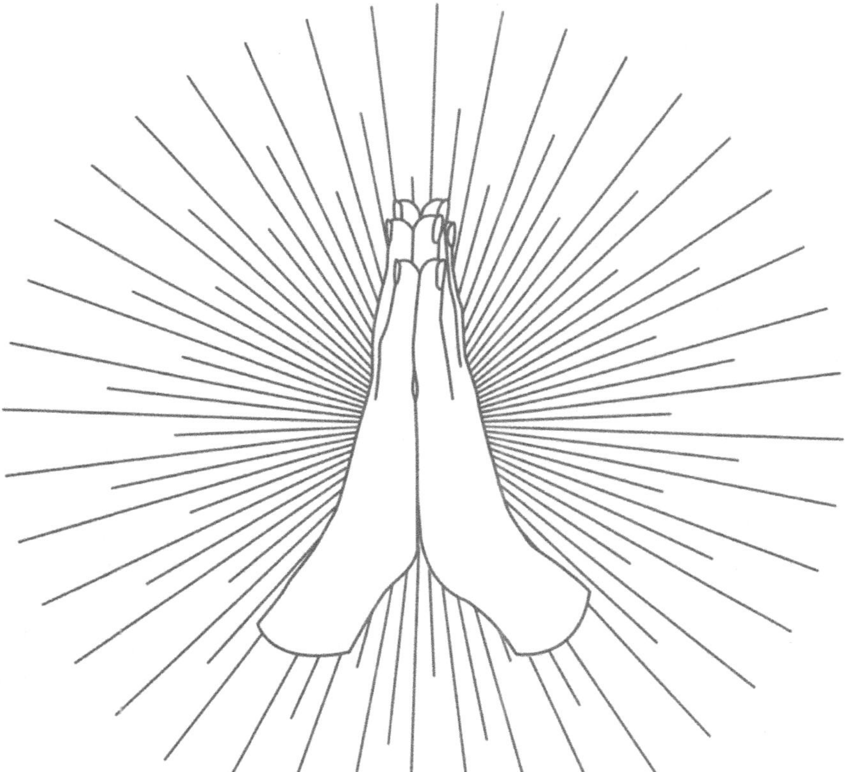

"The divine is not a distant concept but a living presence that we can connect with and draw strength from."

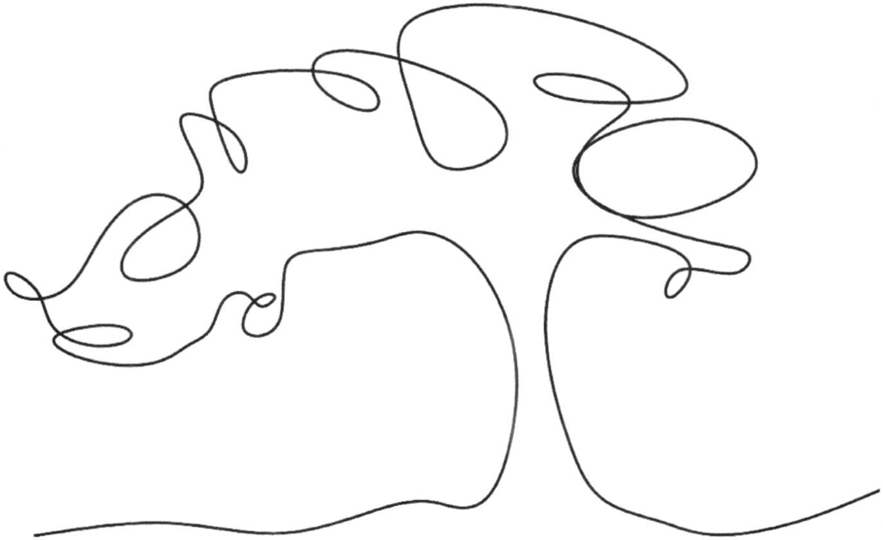

CHAPTER FIVE

Increase Your Own Wealth

The Prosperity Puzzle: Unlocking Financial Abundance

Picture this: a warm, sunny morning, and you're standing at the edge of a lush, sprawling garden. In the center of this garden lies a magnificent tree, its branches heavy with ripe, golden fruits. Each fruit represents a different facet of wealth—financial security, freedom, and the power to turn your dreams into reality.

Welcome to Chapter 5, where we unravel the prosperity puzzle and explore how to increase your own financial wealth. It's a journey that promises to be both practical and enlightening, offering you the keys to unlock the gates of financial abundance.

Financial wealth isn't merely about chasing money for its own sake. It's about wielding the tools of financial wisdom to design a life that you truly desire—a life that's brimming with opportunities, experiences, and the ability to make a difference in the world.

As a 79-year-old who has seen the peaks and valleys of financial fortunes, I can assure you that the pursuit of wealth need not be a blind chase. It can be a mindful, purpose-driven expedition that aligns with your values and aspirations. In these pages, you'll discover the wealth-building principles that have stood the test of time, along with practical strategies to help you take control of your financial destiny.

But remember, financial wealth isn't an isolated journey. It's a thread woven into the tapestry of your life, affecting not only your well-being but also the lives of those around you. It's about creating a positive ripple effect, where your financial prosperity extends to enrich the world in meaningful ways.

So, as we embark on this exploration of financial abundance, imagine yourself plucking those ripe, golden fruits from the tree of prosperity. Open your mind to the possibilities that lie ahead. Embrace the principles of smart financial planning, responsible stewardship, and the art of wealth creation as we unravel the prosperity puzzle together. Your financial wealth is not just about numbers; it's about the life you can create, the dreams you can fulfill, and the positive impact you can make.

What Is WEALTH? Why And How To Increase It?

Wealth determines your level of prosperity, comfort, lifestyle and purchasing or spending power. It is the abundance of valuable resources or possessions that an individual has. It enables you to live a life of your choice.

Wealth is the total of all your assets, movable or immovable, and more importantly, earnings and return thereof monthly or annually. Earnings and returns are very important as they add to your wealth and financial power.

One should review periodically (monthly or quarterly, and then annually) returns on their properties, worth crores of rupees.

It typically encompasses a wide range of assets,

including:

Financial Assets: These include money in bank accounts, investments, stocks, bonds, and other financial instruments.

Real Assets: These consist of physical possessions such as real estate, land, houses, vehicles, and valuable items like art, jewelry, and collectibles.

Business Ownership: Wealth can also be tied to ownership or shares in businesses, which can provide income and capital appreciation.

Income: A high and consistent income can contribute to one's wealth over time, as it allows for savings and investment

Human Capital: The knowledge, skills, and experience a person possesses can also be considered a form of wealth, as it can lead to higher earning potential and career opportunities.

Social Capital: Strong social networks and relationships can be considered a form of wealth, as they can provide opportunities, support, and access to resources.

Educational Attainment: Education and knowledge can be seen as a form of wealth, as they can open doors to higher-paying jobs and career advancement.

Now that we have some wealth, how to increase it further? Are there any time-proven methods or tips?

Let's define our aims:

1 Any investment made should be totally **safe.** There should not be any chance at all of losing any of it.

2 There should be a **reasonable return** on it. Do not be tempted to get high returns and make a risky investment. The capital and money are hard-earned by you; and in no case, any part of it should be lost at all. Safe investments could be Bank (scheduled) Deposits; Government Securities, Gold, real estate, Rentals and Shares of Blue-chip Companies and the like. Make such an investment whose value rises or gives you a return from day 1.

3 Ensure periodic return on your investment as promised by the Investment Agency and market trends. Monitor it regularly.

Now, how to put it into practice? Let's read ahead!

The citizens of the ancient city of Babylon (Iraq/South of Baghdad about 1800 BC) were the most prosperous, in spite of the fact that Babylon had no resources of its own to capitalize on. Then what was the magic?

There were two important inscriptions found in Babylon during its excavation:

1. **Always save 10%** of your earnings and keep it aside safely.
2. **Invest in Gold.**

Let us analyze the above-mentioned points.

10% monthly savings would become 120% after one year, and 360% after 3 years. The figure of 10% saving every month is a manageable amount - it is not very high nor low and, over a period of time, its total becomes significant.

Such savings may be used for emergencies or rainy days your holidays or education and weddings of your loved ones. Some parts of it may also be invested safely.

Many people around the world cleared their debts in a few years with such savings. Thereafter, they started enjoying life by holidaying and having fun. So just tighten your belt slightly and start saving 10% every month from now on. You would enjoy its benefits.

Gold

From time immemorial, glittering gold has always attracted mankind to possess it. Further, its value or cost has always been rising. Gold is often seen as a "safe haven" asset, meaning that it tends to retain or increase its value during times of economic uncertainty or market volatility. Gold is also considered as an investment asset class. Many people and investors buy and hold gold as a way to diversify their investment portfolios and hedge against inflation or economic downturns.

Please see the Table below for prices of gold in India in the last 50 years.

Average Annual Price of Gold (24 Carats per 10 gms.)

	YEAR	Rs. (approx.)	Increase (approx. over the previous figure)
1.	1970	184	Starting Year
2.	1980	1330	x 7.2 (7.2 times)
3.	1990	3200	x 2.4
4.	2000	4400	x 1.4
5.	2010	18500	x 4.2
6.	2020	48651	x 2.63

(From 1970 to 2020, over 50 years, it went up (from 184 to 48651) by 264 times.Source: bankbazaar.com).

Investment in gold has always been safe as it is a precious metal and always has value.

Other Possibilities

Besides, 10% savings and investment in gold, in the present times what are the other options? There appear to be two more.

1. **Real Estate**
2. **Shares of the Blue-chip Cos. (Companies)**

In real estate, one has to be very cautious. Try to go for immediate returns like rental income. Do not fall for any future lucrative schemes. One can't be sure of such schemes.

> **Remember:** *One bird in hand is always better than two in the bush. Even a small amount of monthly rent accumulates into a large amount soon and is far better than idle money. Besides, what you get now could be re-invested to grow further!*

Shares of the Blue-chip Cos.

The Blue-chip Cos. are the top-rated Cos. who never default on their dividend payments and commitments. These Cos. also give bonus shares from time to time to shareholders. It increases the value of your investment.

These Cos. maintain or improve their rank and do not let their reputation suffer even a bit.

In the long run, 5 - 10 years, it gives good returns. Of the **top 50 Nifty Cos.** (National Stock Exchange at

Mumbai - listings of Cos.), you may invest in the Top 50 Nifty Cos. OR choose from among the top 20 to 30 Cos. and invest through your Bank. These days, every bank facilitates investment in shares for its account- holders. Bank has a separate department or division for dealing in shares of various Companies and they keep an eye on the value of shares. They advise regarding the good Cos. and investments in good shares.

Let's summarize:

1. **Save 10%** every month and keep it aside safely.

2. **Invest in Gold** which is fully safe. Gold prices keep rising.

3. **Invest in Real Estate - where you would get monthly rent from day 1.** And not in new proposed construction nor in future lucrative schemes. Monthly rentals would keep increasing your wealth and prosperity enabling you to live a more comfortable and prosperous life.

4. **Invest in Blue-chip Cos.** and grow your wealth.

Increase wealth and lead a prosperous and joyous life with your family. *Remember that building wealth is a gradual process, and there are no shortcuts to substantial financial success. It requires discipline, diligence, and a commitment to making sound financial decisions. It's important to adapt your wealth-building strategies to your specific goals, risk tolerance, and life circumstances. While increasing wealth is a worthy goal, maintaining a balanced and fulfilling life is equally important.*

Always invest safely and
for regular returns.

☆☆☆

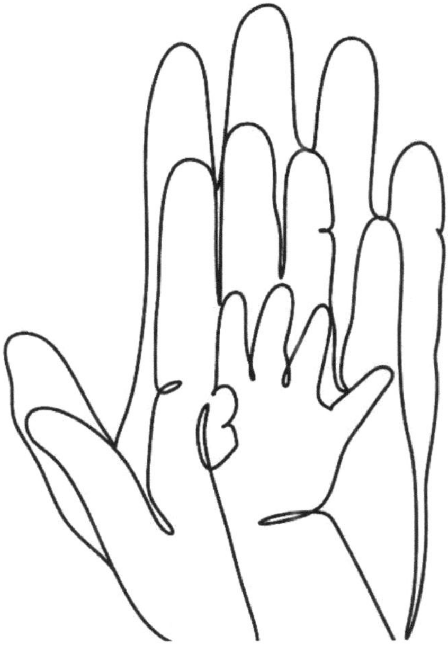

CHAPTER SIX

Interpersonal Relationships

The Dance of Connection

Life is a dance, and at its heart, it's a dance of connection. Each person we meet, and each interaction we have, is a step in this intricate choreography of human relationships. Some steps are graceful and effortless, while others may feel like stumbling through unfamiliar terrain. Yet, it is through this dance that we find meaning, joy, and a profound sense of belonging.

Welcome to Chapter 6, where we dive into the art of interpersonal relationships—the delicate, beautiful, and sometimes challenging dance that we all partake in. In this chapter, we'll explore the steps, rhythms, and melodies that shape our connections with others, and how these relationships can be a wellspring of enduring bliss.

Over the years, I've come to recognize that the quality of our relationships has a profound impact on the tapestry of our lives. Our bonds with family, friends, colleagues, and even acquaintances color the canvas of our existence. They influence our happiness, our growth, and our sense of purpose.

But remember, the dance of connection is not a solo performance; it's a collaborative masterpiece. It's about forging bonds that uplift, support, and inspire. It's about celebrating our shared humanity and the beauty of diversity.

So, as we embark on this exploration of interpersonal relationships, imagine yourself stepping onto the dance floor of life, ready to waltz, tango, and twirl with those who cross your path. Open your heart to the magic of human connection, embrace the rhythms of empathy and understanding, and let this chapter be your guide as we navigate the intricate dance of life's most precious bonds.

You see, everybody wants to have and maintain pleasant and happy relationships with all the people around. It is a scientific fact that even before birth, the human infant has established relationships with the mother, father, family members and those connected with the mother. After birth, the most intimate relationships are with the mother and the father. Breastfeeding brings new closeness as well as comfort and security. Parents are seen as divine, giving sustenance and protection.

As you grow, you come to know your father/guardian, brothers, sisters, etc., and develop a deep bond of love, affection, and friendship with them.

You may like some people more than the rest. *Why?*

Because such people shower more love and affection on you; take more care of you.

You start going to a school, maybe reluctantly! There, you play games and make several friends. The teacher tries affectionately to make you learn a few things through games and songs. You might like some of it. You fall in love with the teacher, the 1st person outside your family. *Why*?

Because of warmth, love and affection showered on you! You would have some good and close friends at the school; and the rest - just known.

At the age of about 15 years and thereafter, one has lots of people around to interact with.

People of your own family — uncles, aunts, and cousins; school friends; teachers, coaches; neighbors; etc.

Do you notice whom you like more and who likes you?

a. Those who have similar thoughts as yours tend to be close! You & they agree mutually most of the time. There is always a pleasant interaction (transaction) with them.

b. You like those who praise you. Everybody likes praise and appreciation. You may win over anybody to your side, maybe for life, by praising him or her or their efforts.

c. Nobody likes criticism. Those who always criticize are kept at arm's length.

Hence, do not criticize and instead, always suggest positive alternatives. Praise others' efforts (give positive strokes).

It has two advantages: the other person won't be offended and it may lead to a better and expeditious solution.

So, for a **good bond** of friendship:

- Get along together and well with others. Have a sweet disposition - be always ready to help others. Do not be unapproachable at all, not even appear to be so.

- Do not criticize; instead offer polite and positive alternatives. Praise the other person (give positive strokes) and he or she will become your lifetime friend. If the matter is not your domain or area of action, do not insist on your views or solution. Let the doer have the freedom to decide and act.

If it is your domain or area of action, note down all the possibilities and coolly consider them all sitting alone or with your team. And you will get the right solution.

Now let's come to our and others' conduct and behavior at any moment for a specific purpose or task.

In this regard, Dr. Eric Berne, a U.S. Psychiatrist, came out with a postulate:

A person's behavior at any moment would fall into one of the following three categories of personality:

- **Parent (P)**: Dominating and commanding like a parent. Also, nurturing, giving warm care and nourishment.
- **Adult (A)**: Reasonable, logical, and responsible like an adult.
- **Child (C)**: Carefree, confused, and ready to follow directions like a child.

The interaction or transaction is between 2 persons or bodies of persons. Let's say X and Y.

P – Parent Mode

As the name suggests, Parent mode is dominating and advising - most of the time.

X (P) is saying to Y(C) - Don't do this or that; that is wrong, do it this way; and so on. Suggesting very strongly:

"I'm okay, you're not okay."

X ought to be cautious here while instructing or directing lest Y gets offended and the relationship is soured. X should be polite and suggestive. The instructions should be very clear and not confusing. Y should respect X and carry out the task as required.

A- Adult Mode

Behavior and conduct of both X and Y are reasonable, logical and mutually acceptable - expressing:

"I'm okay, you're okay."

And the interaction or transaction goes through smoothly and happily for both.

C- Child Mode

X (C) is confused - not knowing what to do and how to go about completing the task at hand! He/she expects guidance and clear directions to do the task properly. Its position is:

"I'm not okay, you're okay."

Parent Y should politely get the task carried out by X (C).

During any interaction or transaction, anyone may shift his/her mode to another mode by changing behavior. Like for instance, C to A or A to P or C to P and the like or vice-versa.

You would notice from the above that the best modes for X and Y are A - A.

X can control its mode and be in the desired mode. But if Y is not in A mode then how to get Y in A mode?

Let's say Y is in P. Then, you X can move from A mode to C mode (opposite of P). Now Y would move from P mode to A mode, and you go back from C to A and complete the transaction happily.

Some examples of daily life are given below to understand the above concept.

Example 1	**Mode**
Student: Please give me the best geometry box.	**A**
Shopkeeper: Here, Rs. 300/-	**P**
Student: But it is labeled Rs. 260/- I'll report you.	**P**
The shopkeeper removes the box and says: We don't have any. You may get it from a downtown market.	**P**
The unsatisfactory end for both.	
Now examine the following transaction.	
Student: Please show me the best geometry box.	**A**
Shopkeeper: Here, Rs. 300/-.	**P**

Student: Uncle *Ji*, we do all our shopping from you and are your regular customer Please don't charge us any extra. **C**

Shopkeeper: Okay. You pay Rs.260/-. **A**

Student: Thank you, Uncle *Ji*. **A**

Transaction satisfactorily concluded.

Example 2	**Mode**
Union Leader (UL) The prices have soared very high. It has become impossible to live with the present wages. We have been requesting you for 2 months to increase the wages by 15%. But nothing has happened, hence the strike. Increase the wages and the strike would be called off.	**P**
Managing Director (MD) The Co. does not have extra funds. Any increase would lead to an increase in the end product price and we shall be out of the market. The Co. would close down. The workers would be jobless. Hence, in the best interest of both, call off the strike and we would continue to explore ways to increase wages.	**P**

UL - First declare an increase in wages, then only the strike shall be called off. **P**

MD - That's not possible. First, withdraw the strike, then we would consider a hike in the wages. **P**

UL - The strike can't be called off unless wages are increased. **P**

Negotiations failed. Unsatisfactory end for both, who remain in P mode only and unfriendly.

Now examine the following transaction:-

Union Leader (UL)

Good morning, Sir. **A**

As the prices have soared very high, it is not possible to live with the present wages. We have been requesting you for 2 months to increase the wages by 15%. But no response was received from your side. Hence, we had to resort to strike. Please tell us about the hike in wages.

Managing Director (MD)

Good morning, Shukla *ji*. **A**

What would you have - tea or coffee?

Tea is ordered and brought in with biscuits.

You know the Chairman was abroad. Hence, we could not respond. Let's examine together what can be done.

We have 200 workers with an average wage of Rs.7200/- per month (pm). **A**

Production: 10,000 bottles p.m.

It comes to 50 bottles per worker pm. Any increase in the wages (plus 20% indirect and overhead cost) would directly affect the price of a bottle, presently Rs. 450/- each.

Let's see the effect of a 5% increase in wages.

5% of Rs.7200 is Rs.360. Plus 20%, it comes to Rs 432/- for 50 bottles, i.e., Rs 8.64 per bottle.

To retain our position in the market, the maximum price increase could be 2%, i.e., Rs 9.00 per bottle.

For 50 bottles, Rs 450/- is the total cost. Wages per worker come to: Rs.450 ÷ 1.2 =Rs. 375/-. It is 5.21% of Rs 7200/-. At best, it could be about 6%, i.e., Rs 430/- per worker.

Please note that none of our competitors has increased the price.

UL: Sir, it is not enough. Kindly make it at least 8%, Rs 576/-. **A**

MD: Let's see its effect on the price. Rs 576 × 1.2 = Rs 691/- for 50 bottles. Per bottle, it comes to Rs 13.82, say, Rs.14. **A**
Total price/ bottle = Rs 450 + 14 = Rs 464/-, about 3% price increase. So, a wage increase of 8% - is it okay, then?

UL: Yes, Sir. Thank you. **A**

MD: And let's increase the monthly production by at least **A**

5%. Okay?

UL: Yes Sir. Thank you. We'll call off the strike now and from tomorrow we will start the work again. **A**

Negotiations successfully concluded.

Both were in A mode throughout friendly and acceptable to each other.

Example 3	Mode
Vegetable Seller (S): Welcome, Madam. *Namaste.*	**A**
I have not seen you for the last 4-5 days, is everything fine?	
House-wife (Buyer): *Namaste.* Yes, all is fine. There was a wedding in the family so we all had been out.	**A**
What are the rates of onions and tomatoes?	
S: Onions - Rs 30 per Kg and tomatoes - Rs 60 per Kg.	**P**
B: Very high. Arre *baba*, last week, these were 20 and 50 only. Please be reasonable, so that we can buy.	**C**
S: What to do, Madam? The prices have soared.	**P**
B: I'll take 5 kg each of - onions at Rs.25 and tomatoes at Rs.55. Okay?	**A**
S: Ma'am, you are our old customer. Okay.	**A**
B: Thank you	**A**

The deal was successfully concluded.

Please note in the above examples two magical words used in successful deals: **'Please' and 'Thank you'.**

These express politeness and regard for the other person.

Do use them often and watch the magic. Always be humble, friendly and polite; and see your tasks getting accomplished.

Similarly, understand the significance of using the following words:

"*Ji*"(in Hindi): Expresses **RESPECT**. Normally used after a name or title, like Esq. in English.

AND used alone to express consent (yes) or to acknowledge.

Sir: One may also use 'Sir' often for the other party during conversation. (Keep your ego aside). And see its magic.

Use Sir/Master/Madam/Miss, appropriately.

Aap*: (in Hindi)**: Means **`You'**, a respectful version, used for elders giving respect to them. In Hindi, the other word for 'you' is '*tum*' - an informal word used normally. This is to suggest always using 'aap***', even for younger ones and see the respect you get.

Remember: *Respect begets respect.*

Namaste: Hindi greeting expressing regards and welcome.

Normally used by younger ones for elders while meeting. The suggestion is to please use it for all people when meeting, even younger ones. And see youngsters picking up this good habit and giving you respect.

Do use often freely and appropriately:

Please/Thank you/Sir/Ji/Madam etc.

We've explored the dynamics between the Parent and Adult modes of interaction—the nurturing and guiding aspects that stem from our caregiving instincts, and the rational, self-aware responses that arise from our Adult selves. Through examples from daily life, we've witnessed how these modes and **being polite can shape our interactions and influence the quality of our relationships and accomplishments.**

As we conclude this chapter, it's essential to recognize that the dance between these modes is not about one being superior to the other. Instead, it's about achieving a delicate balance, a harmonious blend that allows us to engage authentically and effectively with the people in our lives

> **Remember:** *The Parent mode brings warmth, care, and guidance. It's the mode that offers a reassuring hand on the shoulder during challenging times and*

> *celebrates small victories with a heart-warming smile. It's the mode that embodies love, guidance, and protection.*

On the other hand, the Adult mode brings clarity, rationality, and self-awareness. It's the mode that encourages open dialogue, active listening, and constructive problem-solving. It's the mode that seeks mutual understanding and fosters growth.

As we strive to nurture our relationships and deepen our connections, let us remember the lessons of this chapter. Let us be mindful of the modes we engage in and strive to choose the one that best serves the situation. Let us embrace the power of empathy, politeness open communication, and the genuine desire to understand one another.

In the end, the true essence of bliss in our relationships lies in the ability to connect authentically, to love unconditionally, and to grow together. It's about weaving a tapestry of trust, respect, and genuine affection. It's about cherishing the connections that enrich our lives and finding joy in the shared journey.

May the lessons learned in this chapter guide you in crafting heart-to-heart connections that bring lasting happiness, fulfillment, and bliss into your world.

☆ ☆ ☆

Relationships

"Our connections with others are the threads that weave the tapestry of our existence, making life a beautiful and shared masterpiece."

CHAPTER SEVEN

Our Future Generations

Shaping Tomorrow's Responsible Leaders

The future is a vast and unknown terrain, a realm of possibilities and promise that rests in the hands of our children—the inheritors of our world. As we step into the final chapter of our journey towards lasting bliss, we turn our gaze towards the generation that will shape the destiny of our societies, our nations, and our planet.

It's time to embark on a profound exploration of nurturing responsible citizens in our future generations. The lessons and insights shared here transcend personal fulfillment; they extend to the collective well-being of our communities and the sustainability of our world.

Our children are the seeds from which the future will grow. They are the dreamers, thinkers, and innovators who will carry the torch forward. It is our duty and privilege to empower them with the tools, values, and perspectives needed to navigate the challenges and opportunities that lie ahead.

It is imperative that we delve into the art of preparing our youth for the responsibilities of citizenship, not merely as passive observers but as active, engaged participants in shaping a better world. We shall explore strategies to instill values of empathy, responsibility, and social consciousness, ensuring that our future generations are equipped to address the complex issues of time.

But remember, the path to responsible citizenship is not a one-size-fits-all formula. It is a journey that begins with nurturing the individual potential of each young mind, encouraging them to question, to learn, and to contribute in their unique way. It is about fostering an environment that values education, inclusivity, and social awareness.

So, as we commence our exploration of nurturing responsible citizens in our future generations, let us embrace the profound responsibility and privilege that it entails. Together, let us envision a world where the young generation is not just prepared to inherit the future but is actively engaged in building a brighter, more compassionate, and sustainable tomorrow.

Make Them Responsible Citizens!

Children all over are our future generations and they play a crucial role in shaping the future of our societies and the world at large. We must ensure the right development of their character, values, and conduct, viz., **honesty, integrity, patriotism, hard work, loyalty, selflessness, positivity, being organized, planning and helping others.**

The future generation's -impact on the world is significant, and it's influenced by the values, skills, knowledge, and experiences they gain during childhood. By providing children with the necessary tools, guidance, and opportunities, we can help them become responsible, informed, and compassionate individuals who contribute positively to our community.

But how to ingrain and grow them to become responsible citizens? **Well, It would be possible through: NCC.**

Five years of **NCC term, class 8th to 12th** all over the country, would provide, not only the best citizens for the country but also a ready army of volunteers as and when required. It would also lead to a good social life and **curtail anti-social/terrorist activities**.

Above all, they all would have the **National Spirit** (*Rashtriya Bhawana*) placing the nation first and above everything else. It is, sadly, totally missing today.

They will also learn the significance of the 3 Ds—

D

Discipline in their work and life

Determination to reach their goals and meet target

Devotion to the country, welfare of the people and own family.

Presently, it should also be extended to all undergraduate courses of 3 years all over the country, since these students would not have undertaken the NCC.

In the next 5 years or so, the whole complexion and outlook of our young masses would become nationalist, disciplined and objective.

To inculcate Good Habits and Conduct in young ones to follow in Daily Routine

Catch them young - in Schools.

For inculcating good habits among the students, one every year – Class 1 to 12, as suggested below. The Class Teacher is to check & instruct the habit to adopt for that year's class/year daily for a few minutes. It would firmly ingrain in young minds good habits. The Class Teacher would also revise all the previous years' habits adopted as per the guidelines. Like in Class 4, the habit advised is "to look after your things well & they will serve you well". The Teacher would also revise the previous 5 years' habits advised. Similarly, in class 12th all the previous 13 years' habits would be revised daily.

Guidelines for Nursery 1 to Classes 12.

Class	Guideline/Habit
Nursery 1.	*Obey and respect your Parents.*
Greet them every morning with folded hands -*Namaste* or other appropriate greeting.	
Nursery 2.	*Always speak the truth and be honest.*

Class 1

- ***Always be neat and tidy, head to toe.***
- *Keep your surroundings clean.*
- Daily clean your teeth (twice - morning and at bedtime).
- Take a bath daily and groom your hair well.

- Ensure your nails are cut. And shoes polished. Whenever and wherever you go, be smart, well-dressed and well-mannered.
- *Always carry a handkerchief* wherever you go.

Class 2

- ***Do daily your school homework without fail.***

Class 3

- Play while you play and study while you study.
- ***Whatever you do, do it with full (100%) involvement and concentration.***

Class 4

- ***Look after your things well and they will serve you well.*** Like pens, pencils, notebooks, books, clothes, your money purse.

Class 5

- ***Always help others*** to the extent possible for you.

Class 6

- ***Respect your teachers and elders.*** Greet them appropriately.

Class 7

- ***A place for everything and everything in its place.*** At home, in the workplace, in your bag and everywhere else, follow the above.

Class 8

- ***Time for everything and everything on time.*** Decide all the activities you want to do and allot time for every activity. Like playing games, watching TV, doing school homework, pursuing hobbies, and undertaking special coaching or training. Reading good books/magazines, and the like. And do every activity on time.

Class 9

- ***Always have a POSITIVE attitude and outlook in all matters.***

Class 10

- ***To go to heaven, you yourself have to die.*** Nobody else can do it for you. This is to say that work so hard yourself as if you are dying. It would get you good results to be elated (like being in heaven).

Class 11

- ***Have full faith & trust in the Creator/the Almighty.*** He has created you and this Universe. Pray daily to Him to keep you and your loved ones well, healthy, and happy.

Class 12

- ***Do things ahead of time.*** And not at the 11th hour, to avoid unnecessary pressure and ensure the work got done properly.

IIT-Kanpur Education Pattern — To Produce Thinkers And Problem-Solvers

The IIT-Kanpur graduates for over the past 50 years (1st batch came out in 1965) have made an impact all over the world, reaching top positions of reputed organizations.

*What was the magic of producing such "**Thinkers**" and "**Problem Solvers**"!*

It was the Education Pattern adopted at IIT-Kanpur in its formative years, 1960 - 1970, under the dynamic leadership of its 1st Director,

Dr.PK Kelkar (Padam Bhushan).

He was also instrumental in winning over the US Delegation to agree to aid IIT-Kanpur in higher Technological Education.

Essential Traits required in a graduate of IIT-Kanpur were identified as:

i. **THINK** independently and freely.
ii. Be **REGULAR**.
iii. Understand and follow well the **BASICS** and **FUNDAMENTALS.**
iv. Know how to deal with **ACTUAL LIFE** and the **OUTSIDE WORLD.**
v. **LOOK AROUND** to know and learn the latest.

How To Achieve The Above?

At first, it appears difficult to inculcate such traits in actual practice but simple and effective measures were adopted. And the results were there for everybody to see. These measures, to my understanding, were:

- No preparatory leaves for the exams and tests.
- Surprise tests.
- Open book examinations.
- All questions in any examination paper were new, none previously worked out, seen, or tried.
- Weightage for the assignments, mid-term tests, practicals, etc.
- Tutorial classes in undergraduate classes.

- One Humanities course is compulsory in every semester.
- Practical aspects of all Theories.
- Having full trust in people.
- Open system of education and learning.
- Exposure to the latest in Science and Technology.

In the 1960s at IIT-K, students knew about lasers, facsimiles, and satellite communication, besides color TV and computers, of course. (Next para)

If the above measures are adopted in our education pattern all over the country, it would turn out thinkers everywhere, bringing more prosperity to our people.

As we conclude our journey through the pages of this book and specifically as we finish the final chapter on nurturing responsible citizens in our future generations, let us reflect on the significance of this endeavor.

Our world is in a constant state of flux, facing a multitude of challenges that require thoughtful, responsible, and compassionate individuals to address. The future is not a distant abstraction; it is being shaped by the values, knowledge, and actions of our youth today.

In this chapter, we have explored strategies and ideas to guide our children towards responsible citizenship, encouraging them to become active participants in the betterment of society. We have emphasized the importance of education, social consciousness, and fostering an environment that values empathy and responsibility.

But beyond the practical advice lies a deeper truth—that the legacy we leave behind is not measured solely by our personal accomplishments but by the impact we have on the generations that follow. It is in nurturing responsible, compassionate, and engaged citizens that we sow the seeds of a brighter and more harmonious future.

So, as you turn the final page of this book and step back into the world, remember that the journey towards lasting bliss is not a solitary one. It is a journey that we undertake collectively, as a community of individuals striving to create a better world for ourselves and for generations yet to come.

May the thoughts shared in these pages serve as a guidepost on your path to a more fulfilling and purposeful life. May it inspire you to embrace the challenges of times with courage and empathy; and may it empower you to play your part in nurturing responsible citizens in future generations. In doing so, you contribute to a legacy that transcends your own existence, leaving a mark of enduring significance on the tapestry of humanity.

☆ ☆ ☆

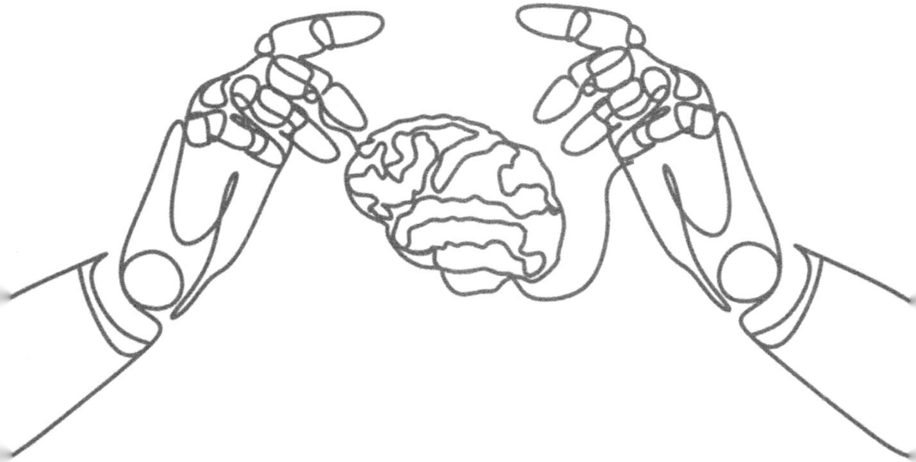

"The legacy we leave is not in what we accumulate but in how we empower and inspire the generations that follow."

Conclusion

As we arrive at the concluding page of our book on living in bliss, it's time to reflect on the transformative journey we've undertaken.

In closing this book, let us remember that the pursuit of lasting bliss is not a passive endeavor. It is a call to action, an invitation to live with purpose and intention, and a commitment to make a positive impact on our lives and the lives of those around us.

Having traversed the vast landscape of life, I can assure you that bliss is not a distant, unattainable dream. It is a reality within your grasp, a state of being that you can nurture and cultivate every single day.

The wisdom shared within these pages is not meant to be shelved and forgotten; it is meant to be lived. It is an invitation to embrace the present moment, connect with the divine, cultivate your inner sanctuary, navigate the complexities of financial wealth, dance with authenticity in your relationships, and empower our future generations.

Let this book be a catalyst for positive change in your life. Let it inspire you to take the first step, no matter how small, towards a more blissful existence. Let it encourage you to foster compassion, kindness, and empathy in your interactions with others. Let it empower you to make responsible choices that contribute to a better world.

Remember that bliss is not a destination; it is a journey. It is a journey filled with moments of joy, challenges, growth, and transformation. It is a journey that unfolds day by day, and it is a journey that you are fully capable of embracing.

Living in bliss is not about a life free of challenges, but rather one filled with the wisdom to navigate those challenges with grace. It is not about perpetual happiness but rather a sustained state of well-being rooted in authenticity, connection, and purpose.

It is your birthright, and it resides within you. You have the capacity to create a life filled with joy, meaning, and fulfillment. Your journey to living in bliss is a journey to reclaim your true self, savor the beauty of each moment, and share the light of your bliss with the world.

Living in bliss is not an ideal to reach but a journey to embrace. It is your journey, and it is the most profound and fulfilling journey you can undertake. So, with a heart full of gratitude and a spirit renewed with purpose, step forth onto your path of bliss.

So, as you close this book, do not let it be the end, but rather, let it be the beginning of a new chapter in your life—a chapter filled with purpose, meaning, and an unwavering commitment to living in bliss, not just for today, but for all the days that follow.

Embrace the journey. Embrace the possibilities. Embrace the bliss that is yours to discover, nurture, and share with the world. The power is within you, and the time is now. Go forth, my dear reader, and live a life of enduring bliss.

Your journey is yours to craft, and the pages of your life's story are yet to be written. May your life be a testament to the blissful existence you deserve.

About The Author

After leaving his legacy at IIT Kanpur, the author Gyanesh Chaudhry, was one of the few who joined the Electronics R & D Division of Tata Electric Cos., in Bombay in October 1967. His vision and foresight facilitated them to build up and establish the new division from scratch, besides carrying out the new projects successfully. His indomitable fervor for his work made him win "Under Frequency Detection System & Gradual Load Shedding " as the best annual project by FICCI in the 1970s.

His other prestigious credentials also include the Amity University Awards of Corporate Excellence & HR Excellence (2008), the National Award in Lean Manufacturing Techniques by the Ministry of MSME (2013), the National Award in Innovation by the Ministry of MSME (2014), and Winner of Excellence Award in Cost Competitiveness by ASSOCHAM India (2015).

NOTES

Date | **Reference Page**

NOTES

Date	Reference Page